MW00770960

Dedication

Many thanks to Gary Marlatt, master rod builder and instructor; Ritch Phillips, who unveiled the mysteries of the macro lens; and "Gipper" Stinson, who patiently deciphered my scrawl and typed the manuscript.

DO IT YOURSELF ROD BUILDING

By Bill Stinson

Photos by the author

Frank Amato Publications, Inc.
PO Box 82112 • Portland, Oregon 97282

CONTENTS

CHAPTER 1

General Remarks

U NTIL RECENTLY, IT WAS difficult to obtain good rod blanks and rod building components. For the most part the blanks that were offered were not the rod manufacturer's best effort.

The available blanks were one piece affairs that, because of their long lengths, the world's transporters of merchandise found difficult to ship. Once the eager rod builder was able to lay his hands on a rod blank he had to make an agonizing decision. Either he would leave it in one piece and contend with the subsequent difficulties of transporting a long, one piece rod or cut it into two or more sections for greater portability.

If the blank was cut, the options were few. Most opted to fit a metal ferrule to the blank. A metal ferrule will join a rod together and is the method used to join today's cheap fiberglass rods. Also, because of the lack of any other method the metal ferrule is the instrument used to unite the sections of most bamboo, cane, and greenheart rods.

One of the major problems with metal ferrules is that they

create a flat spot in a rod's action. They also deaden the inherent sensitivity of the rod's blank. It is much more difficult to detect a delicate strike if this oftentimes miniscule sensation has to pass through a metal ferrule.

Metal ferrules are also heavy and bulky and detract from the esthetics of a well-crafted rod.

At the point where the metal ferrule joins with the fiberglass or other plastic rod material, there will be considerable stress because of the dissimilarity of the two materials. The metal flexes but slightly and the plastic bends a great deal. This contrast in degree of flexibility creates a major weak spot in the finished rod.

Another type of ferrule is called the spigot ferrule. This type is constructed by gluing a piece of fiberglass or graphite to the inside of the blank where the two sections are joined. The spigot very readily lends itself to the building of multi-piece rods and some of today's best travel rods use this system.

Recently, some of the best rod manufacturer's have made their top quality blanks available to the custom rod builder and to the do-it-yourselfer. One manufacturer goes so far as to print a cross reference chart in his blank catalog to indicate which blanks go into their finished rods. The accessibility of these self-ferruled blanks make it practical for both the amateur or professional rod builder to assemble a finished rod far superior to most of the mass produced models on the market. The tip over butt self-ferruled blanks have actions equivalent to one piece blanks.

The availability and ease of shipment of the two piece blanks prompted both sporting goods dealers and mail order houses to seek out and stock top quality rod components. A wide selection of excellent guides, handle materials, thread, finish and tools is readily available.

It is now possible to build beautiful, custom quality rods with very few tools. Chances are that the reader will have most of the required implements lying around the house. The elaborate electric power wrapping machines do not produce a better rod but they do speed up the production rate of the professional.

There are several incentives to building one's own rod. First, is cost. A perusal of a popular fishing tackle catalog that offers both the finished rods and the rod blanks from the same manufacturer indicates that one can save about a third of the purchase price of a factory produced rod if he chooses to buy the materials and assemble it himself. Second, is the desire to create something a little different than is available "off the shelf." The artistic nature of some may be quite different from the rod designer employed by the manufacturer. Third, there is a lot of pride in having done it yourself. Some folks just like to fish with rods that they have self-created.

The first decision to make when building a rod is the selection of the rod blank. The blank is the heart and soul of the rod and regardless of the amount of work and skill that goes into the building, a fine rod is not going to emerge unless a top quality blank is used. Absolutely, avoid the barrel of scuffed seconds that some dealers offer. These are easily recognizable because they will not be identified with a manufacturer's name. Seconds are not available in guides, reel seats, thread, or handles so if one of these cheap blanks is bought, the first line components will be wasted.

Rod blank manufacturers provide elaborate catalogs that give complete specifications for the products that they produce.

The warranty that the manufacturer puts on his blank is very important. Some manufacturers offer no warranty at all. If the blank breaks, the builder is stuck. If there is a warranty, it is usually printed in the manufacturer's catalog. An inquiry to the dealer will indicate which blanks are offered under warranty.

The writer suggests that the first rod be built on a high quality fiberglass blank. The construction method of building graphite or boron rods is essentially the same as glass. A glass blank will be less expensive but can be made into a fine fishing rod. After all the techniques have been learned, then a more expensive graphite or boron blank can be used. The amateur's first attempt should end up better than most mass produced rods available over the counter, as long as first rate materials are utilized. Many mass produced rods are finished by very unskilled personnel who are working against the clock in some distant land.

Determine the type rod you want to make and then refer to pages 72, 73 and 74 to find out about guide spacing and guide sizes. Complete tables are included for a great variety of rods.

The charts in this book will give some suggestions of average guide spacing and guide sizes. A knowledgeable dealer can also be a big help in the selection of the guides, handles, and reel seats. A rough rule of thumb is that a light action rod will require more guides than a heavier action rod. Light actioned rods also require guides of very light weight. If heavy duty guides are used, the blank will be overloaded and the action deadened. Stiffer actioned rods that have very light tips will require closer spacing of guides on the tip. Guides perform the function of keeping the line away from the rod blank thus reducing friction and facilitating casting.

Many improvements have been made in guides during the last few years. The finish of conventional guides has been improved by hard chrome. Ceramic guides and tip tops are very durable and smooth and greatly reduce line wear and friction.

As we come to the various chapters on the individual types of rods, guides suitable for a particular type of rod will be discussed in more detail. Before any thread is applied to the blank, the guides should be taped to the shaft to insure proper spacing.

In the first attempt a pre-formed handle is suggested.

Modern nylon rod wrapping thread is available in a wide selection of sizes and colors. The sizes used in rod wrapping vary from the smallest size (00) to the largest size (EE). The following chart will give the approximate size and strength of the various threads.

Designated Size	Pound Test	Wraps Per Inch
00	2.0	160
A	3.0	120
B	3.5	110
D	6.0	90
E	9.0	70
EE	13.0	60

Size 00 is used for the very lightest rods and also for the wrapping trim.

Size A is popular for most freshwater rods.

B is a good choice for the heavier freshwater and light saltwater models.

Medium saltwater rods will finish nicely with size D.

E and EE are reserved for the very heaviest sturgeon and saltwater rods.

Thread should always be stored in a clean box or plastic bag and handled with clean hands if its color and strength is to be maintained.

Large diameter thread will require more finishing material to adequately cover it and will add weight and bulk to a rod. Unnecessary weight will tend to deaden the action of lightweight blanks.

The pound test of the thread is of little concern when the rod is being wrapped. If size 00 breaks during the wrapping process, too much tension is being used. A good measure of proper tension is to attempt to move the guide after the thread is in place. The wrap should be loose enough so that the guide can be moved slightly during the final alignment process. At the same time if sufficient tension is not used the guide will flop out of place before the finish is applied. The strength of the wrap is obtained by the large number of thread turns. Small, smooth, nicely tapered guide feet can be neatly covered by a small diameter thread. Big guide feet require large thread to adequately cover them. It is essential that the builder sight down the rod to make sure all the guides are in line with the tip top and reel seat before any finish is applied to the wrappings.

When the finish material is applied, the thread will tend to darken. If the original thread color is to be maintained, a color preserver must be used. A coat or two of the preserver will set the color of the thread and subsequent coats of the final finish will not darken it. The major disadvantage of using color preservers is that most of them form a coating on top of the wrap and prevent the final finish from penetrating through the thread to the rod blank. The strongest wraps are obtained when the epoxy finish is applied directly to the thread and the color preserver is eliminated.

There is a thread available called NCP, which stands for "No Color Preserver." This thread maintains its color without the use of color preserver. Its main disadvantage is that appearance of the final wrap is somewhat dull and flat.

For many years about the only form of finish available for rod wrappings was some form of spar varnish. Several coats of this venerable material made a reasonably durable thread covering. In time however, it would check and crack and the rod would have to be stripped, rewrapped, and refinished.

The modern polymer or epoxy rod finishes are extremely durable and should last the lifetime of the guides. Their formulas provide an extremely durable yet flexible thread covering. Good results demand that the manufacturer's mixing and curing instructions be followed exactly. The amount of epoxy applied to the thread will depend on the rod builder's taste. Some prefer to set the thread with one thin coating so that slight ridges and valleys occur on each filament of thread. Others apply two or three heavy coatings that produce a deep translucent covering. Too heavy a coating on the wraps of a light actioned rod will overload a lightweight blank.

The basic difference in building various types of rods is in the construction of the handle. Wrapping the guides and applying the finish to the thread is essentially the same for all rods.

Once the skills of wrapping the guides and gluing the pre-formed components of the handle are mastered, it is easy to build several types of rods.

The more adventuresome can purchase cork rings and either lathe turn them or hand file and sand them to the desired shape.

Handle kits that contain all the necessary parts for a particular type of rod are now available. These kits greatly speed the assembly of the rod. Parts are easily trimmed to fit the individual desire of the rod builder.

CHAPTER 2

Preparation of the Blank and Guides

The first step in preparing a new rod blank is cleaning it. A vigorous rubdown with a clean towel will usually do the job. If the blank has been handled a great deal, a scrubbing with soap and warm water may be necessary. If a gummed price label is difficult to remove, lighter fluid or lacquer thinner will remove all traces.

Rod blanks have a spine or stiff side. In order to find and identify the spine, wrap a piece of masking tape a couple of inches from the rod tip. Place the butt of the tip section on a smooth, level surface. At a point three or four inches from the tip, cradle the blank in the first joint of the index finger of one hand. Place the fingers of the other hand on the middle of the blank and apply enough pressure to form a bow. Slowly rotate the blank. The blank will "jump" into a pronounced bend. This is the spine.

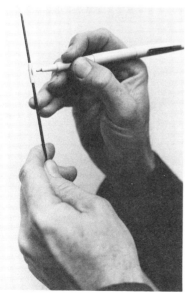

Carefully, mark the direction of the bow on the masking tape. The same technique is used on one piece blanks. The butt section of most two piece blanks is usually sufficiently stiff that it will be difficult or impossible to find the spine. It is usually not necessary to locate the spine on the butt section.

The guides will either be placed in line with the spine or on its reverse side.

Before any gluing is done, assemble all parts on the blank. Tape on the tip top and guides in line with the spine. Some blanks will have a slight curve that is usually in line with the spine. The weight of the guides will frequently straighten the blank. If the weight of the guides increases the degree of the curve in the blank, the guides should be moved 180 degrees to the opposite side of the spine.

CHAPTER 3

Spinning Rods

T HE NECESSARY MATERIALS to build a spinning rod
   include a rod blank, butt cap, rear grip, reel seat, fore
grip, winding check, hook keeper (optional), guides, thread,
tip top, thread finish, masking tape, regular epoxy cement,
and five minute epoxy.

The required tools for a cork grip fishing rod are a coarse
round file, 8 inches of monofilament fishing line, razor blade,
acetone, and a small brush for applying finish. If the outside
of the cork is to be shaped, then a rough rasp and coarse,
medium and fine sandpaper will be necessary.

The only tools needed to build a rod with a foam handle
are a razor blade, acetone, monofilament and a small brush.

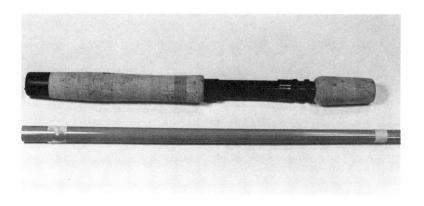

Lay the handle components alongside the rod blank to indicate the portion of the blank that will be covered by the
handle. Mark this portion with a piece of masking tape.

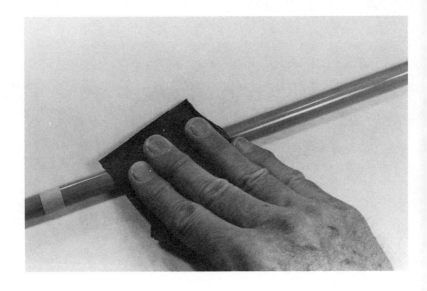

Lightly sand the area that will be covered by the handle. The sanding will provide a good bonding surface for the epoxy. Too vigorous a sanding may damage some of the fibers in the blank.

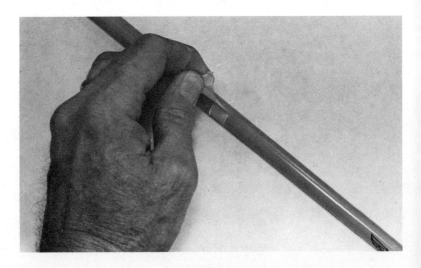

Remove the masking tape and wipe the blank clean.

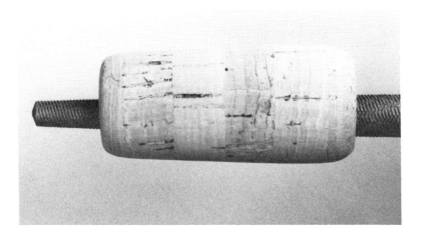

Ream out the fore and rear sections of cork until they will slide easily to the desired position on the blank. Be sure to remove cork equally from all sides so that the cork handle will be centered on the blank. The file can also be used to score the inside of the reel seat. Epoxy adheres best if the smooth metallic surface has been roughened.

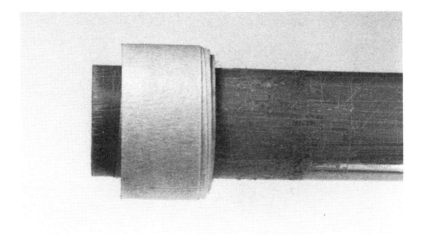

If the butt cap does not fit snugly on the blank, a few turns of masking tape will fill in the gap.

Slide the rear grip up to the butt cap. When the fit is good, apply a generous amount of epoxy cement to the masking tape and inside the butt cap and join together.

Next apply epoxy to the portion of the blank that will be covered by the rear grip and slide the cork into place.

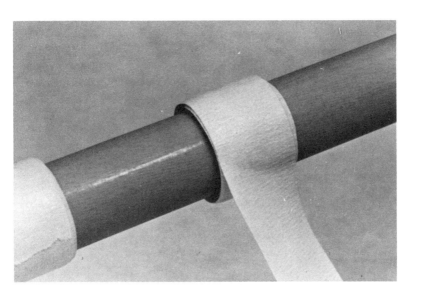

Wrap three sleeves of masking tape around the blank to insure a snug fit of the reel seat. Cork bushings can be purchased that accomplish the same purpose.

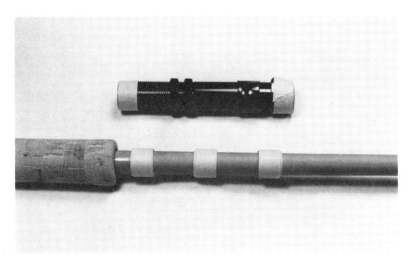

A covering of masking tape on the ends of the reel seat will protect it.

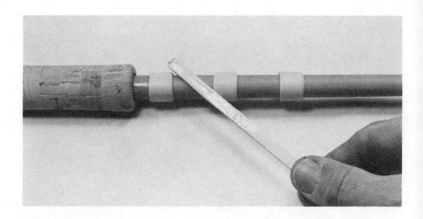

Spread a generous amount of regular epoxy on the masking tape and rod blank and slide on the reel seat. Whether the reel seat threads are in an up or down position is up to the individual.

If the blank is one piece, make sure the reel seat is aligned with the future position of the tip top.

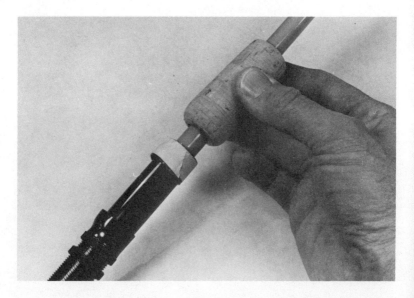

Add epoxy to the portion of the blank to be covered by the fore grip and slide on the cork.

Remove the protective tape from the reel seat. With a clean rag dipped in acetone remove any surplus epoxy before it has a chance to dry.

Dab a little epoxy on the cork and blank that will be covered by the winding check.

Slide on the winding check.

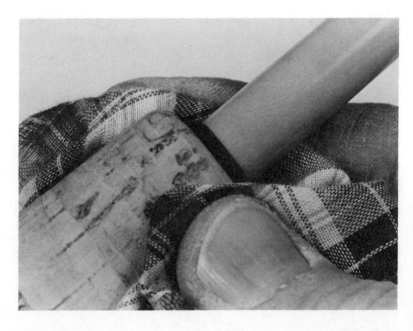

Wipe off the surplus epoxy. Allow the glue to dry and the handle is complete.

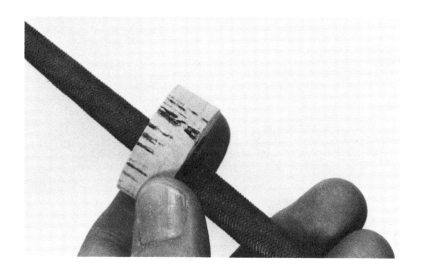

If a rod handle design is desired that is not available in pre-
formed cork or foam, 1/2-inch cork rings can be used. The
corks are reamed out with a round file or cork rasp until they
fit snugly on the blank. Fit all cork rings on the blank before
applying any glue. Write a number on the outside edge of
each ring to insure the proper sequence when reassembling
the handle in the gluing process.

Apply glue to the portion of the blank that will be covered
by the cork and slip on a cork ring.

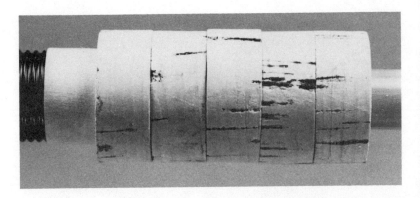

Apply glue to the side of the cork ring and slide on the next ring. Glue must be applied to each side of the rings to insure maximum strength.

Wrap masking tape on the adjacent blank and reel seat to prevent scuffing during the shaping and sanding process.

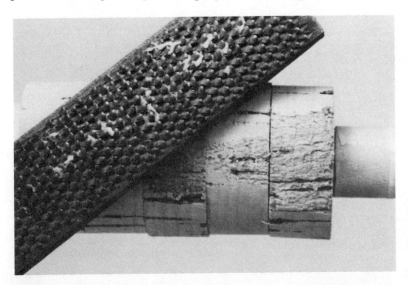

After the epoxy has dried overnight, the handle may be shaped with a rasp. If you are fortunate enough to have access to a wood turning lathe, the handle can be power turned. If not, a good job can be done by hand. Be careful to take the cork down evenly on all sides.

After the desired shape is attained, begin the smoothing process with coarse sandpaper. Again, be sure to sand evenly on all sides. Proceed to medium and fine grits and finish with very fine.

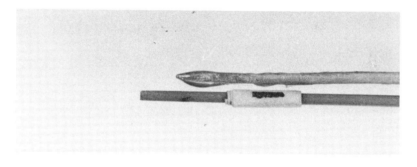

Several adhesives are available that can be used to affix the tip top to the blank. One consideration is that if the tip top becomes damaged it will have to be replaced. Ferrule cement has frequently been used for this purpose. It is easy to use and the heat of a match melts it. It usually holds. Unfortunately, on two occasions I have had a ferrule-cement-secured tip top come loose while fighting a fish. It is very unnerving to watch part of your rod go sliding down the line. After the second unfortunate occurrence, I quit using the stuff. Regular two part epoxy cement will really secure a tip top. In fact, the tip top may be in place forever; broken or not. Five minute epoxy works very well for holding tip tops. It sets rapidly and with the heat of a candle can be removed if replacement is necessary.

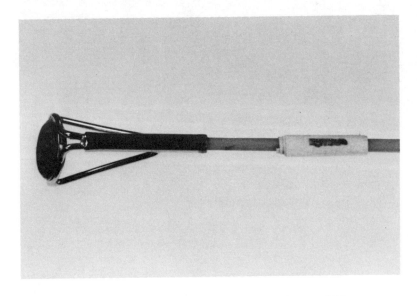

The tip top will be placed in line with the spine or 180 degrees away from the spine. Ceramic tip tops are very durable and slick. The good quality brands are almost impossible to groove or wear out.

Ceramic guides have become very popular on spinning rods. Double footed guides are more durable than the single footed variety. However, the single footed guides allow the blank to flex and are lighter.

Light actioned blanks require lightweight guides. Both the Foul Proof and single foot guides have this characteristic.

CHAPTER 4

Ultra Light Spinning Rods

T O INSTALL THE HANDLE of an ultra light rod that utilizes sliding rings, the first step is to lightly sand the portion of the blank that will be covered by the cork. Next, ream out the cork with a round file.

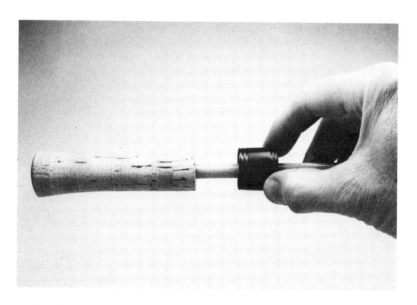

Cut the cork handle into two sections and slip a sliding ring onto each section.

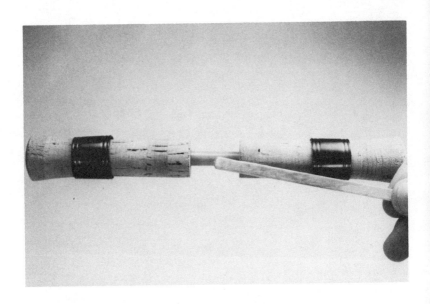

Apply a generous quantity of regular epoxy to the rod blank and to the faces of the two sections of cork.

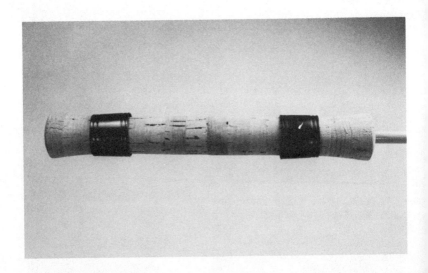

Slide the two sections of cork together and snug up tight. Wipe off any surplus epoxy. A light sanding of the glued joint may be necessary.

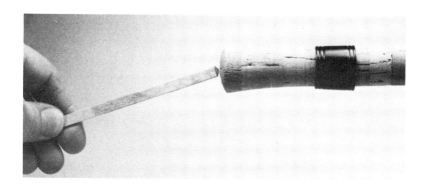

Some sort of plug should be used to cover the end of the blank. A pencil eraser or a piece of dowel may be used on small blanks or the hole can be filled with a mixture of five minute epoxy and cork dust.

CHAPTER 5

Synthetic Foam Handles for Boat and Spinning Rods

L IGHTWEIGHT SYNTHETIC foam handles have become very popular because of their comfort, durability, gripability and ease of assembly. This new material represents a big improvement over the old hypolon material that was very heavy. Foam handles are very desirable for boat and spinning rods. Because of its durability this material should be used for the handle of any rod that will spend much time in a rod holder.

The accompanying illustrations show the installation of a typical boat or saltwater handle. Note the graphite and stainless steel reel seat. This seat is very strong, lightweight and resistant to saltwater.

On a rod utilizing a foam handle, the portion of the blank that will be covered by the foam should not be sanded before assembly. Sanding may make it difficult to push the clinging material down the blank. Before gluing, slide the handle down the blank from the tip end with light pressure. Do not force it or it might become stuck.

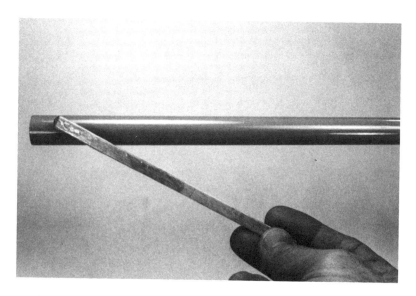

If the grip slides to within a few inches of the end, remove it and apply a light coating of regular epoxy to the portion of the blank that will be covered by the grip.

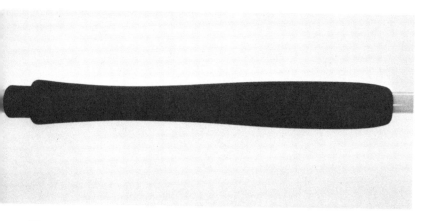

The epoxy acts as a lubricant and with a little pushing the handle should slide down to the end giving a nice snug fit.

If the hole in the handle is a bit too small, boiling the foam in water for ten or fifteen minutes will cause the handle to expand a little.

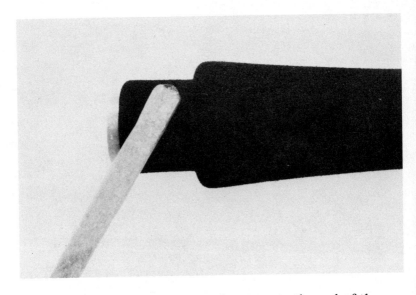

When the rear grip is in place, apply epoxy to the end of the foam grip.

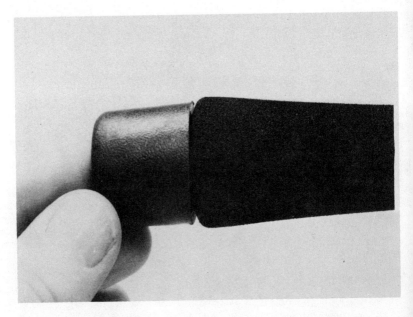

Slide on the butt cap.

34

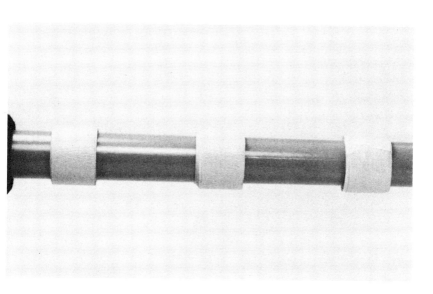

Build up the area under the reel seat with masking tape.

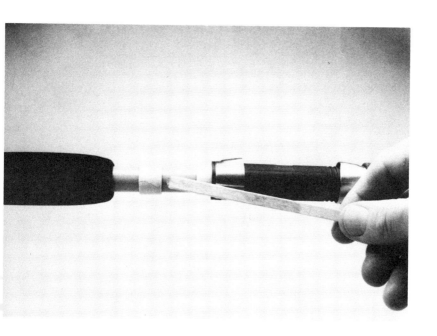

Apply a generous amount of epoxy.

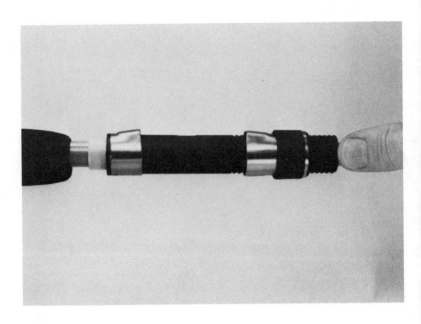

Slide on the reel seat. If the rod is one piece, be sure the reel seat is aligned properly with the blank's spine.

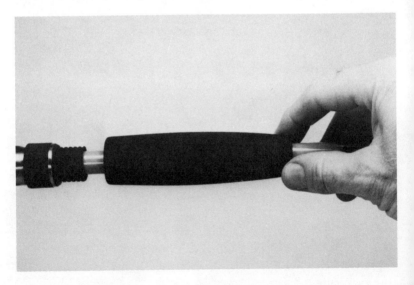

After applying epoxy to the blank, slide the fore grip until it butts up against the reel seat.

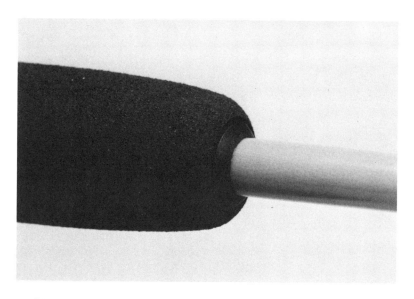

Glue on a winding check and the handle is finished.

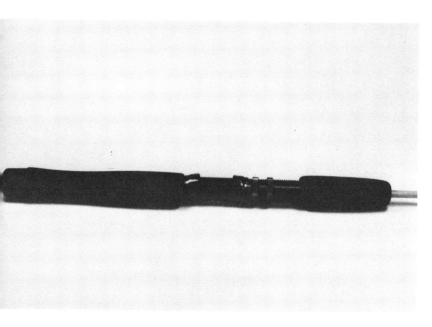

This photo illustrates a typical foam handle on a spinning rod.

CHAPTER 6

Steelhead Rods

U NTIL PRE-FORMED HANDLE kits came along, the cork covered reel seats that are so popular on steelhead rods were a project reserved for only the expert rod builder.

These kits enable the do-it-yourselfer to build a fine custom handle.

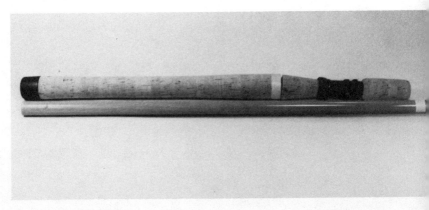

The first step is to mark off the portion of the blank that will be covered by the handle.

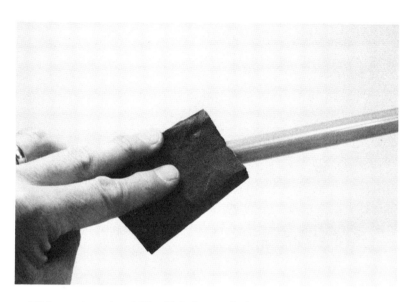

This section should be lightly sanded.

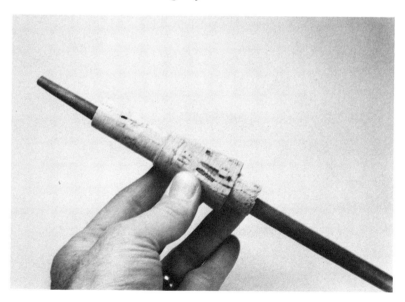

Ream out all of the cork components so that they slide onto their assigned positions on the blank. Remove the cork evenly from all sides of the bore.

The cork that surrounds the metal hood of the reel seat is cut out with a very sharp knife. A covering of masking tape will prevent the cork from splitting.

The metal hood should be flush or slightly below the level of the cork.

Assemble all components on the blank to make sure everything fits.

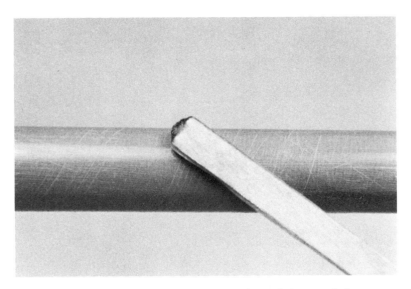

Apply regular epoxy to the butt section of the sanded part of the blank and slide on the rear portion of the handle.

Apply epoxy to the cork that will be under the butt cap.

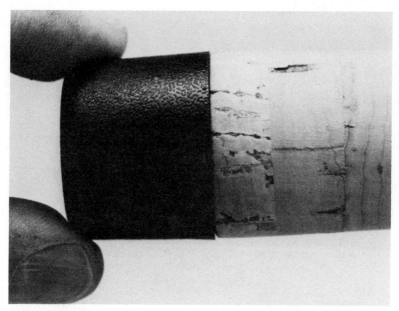

Slide on the butt cap.

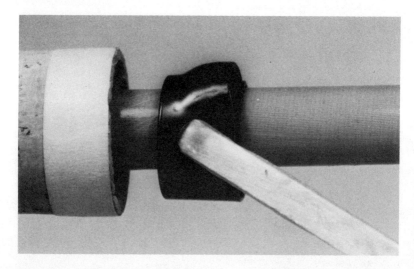

Apply epoxy to the outside of the metal hood and ease the hood into the hollowed out cork. Because this portion of the rod will be subjected to rigorous pressure by the cavorting steelhead, plenty of epoxy is in order.

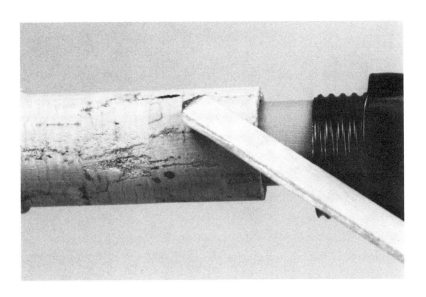

Apply epoxy to the cork that goes inside the hood. Do not forget to smear epoxy on the blank under the cork.

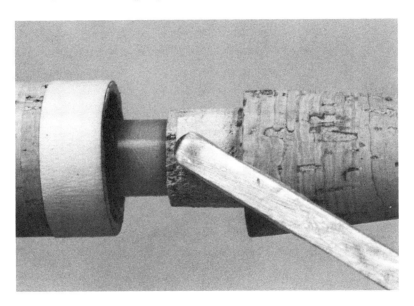

Cover the cork that fits under the threaded part of the reel seat with epoxy. Slip the threaded barrel into place.

43

Dab epoxy on the blank.

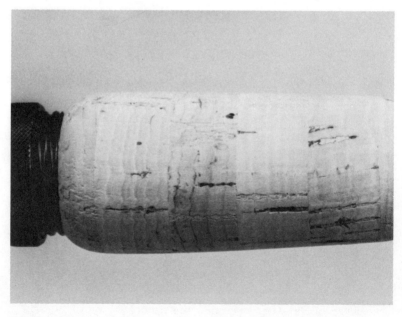

Slide on the fore grip.

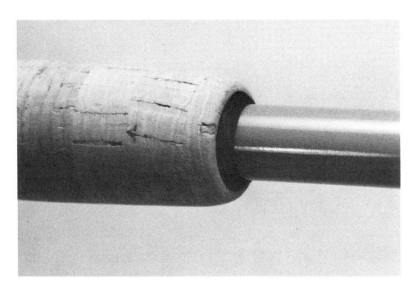

Glue on a winding check.

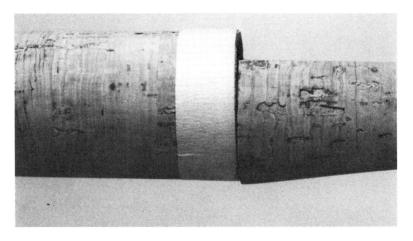

Remove the masking tape and thoroughly wipe off any excess glue.

After the epoxy has dried, a little sanding where the cork sections join will finish the job. Wrap the exposed metal parts of the reel seat with tape to prevent scuffing. When sanding cork start out with a fairly coarse grit and gradually work down to a 400 texture sandpaper.

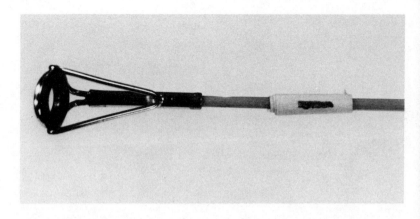

Ceramic tip tops are the accepted standard for steelhead rods.

The tips of steelhead blanks should be sensitive and flexible. Small, light, ceramic guides will not overload these light tips.

CHAPTER 7

Fly Rods

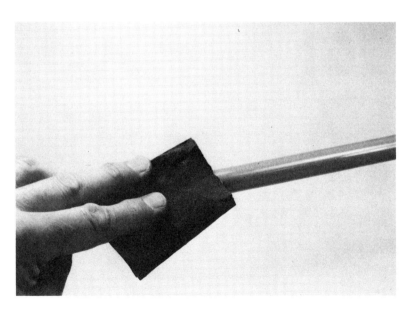

Begin building your fly rod by lightly sanding the portion of
the blank that will be covered by the reel seat and cork
handle.

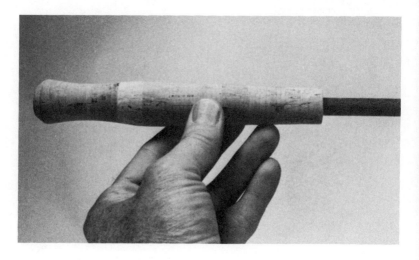

Ream out the cork grip until it slides easily down the blank to its assigned position. Remove cork evenly from all sides of the bore.

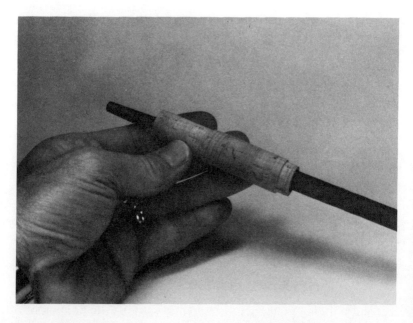

If a cork bodied reel seat has been selected, ream out the cork until it fits the butt end of the blank.

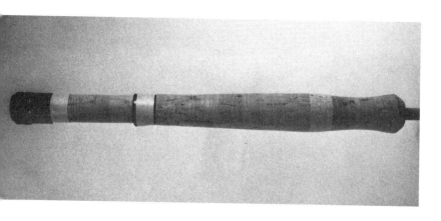

Assemble all parts of the handle and reel seat on the blank before any gluing is undertaken.

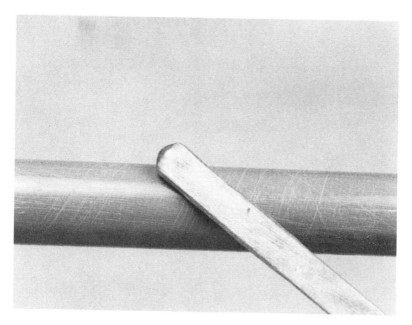

Apply regular epoxy to the portion of the blank to be covered by the reel seat.

Whether the reel seat is to be installed with threads up or down depends upon the individual preference of the angler.

Slide the cork barrel down the blank into position.

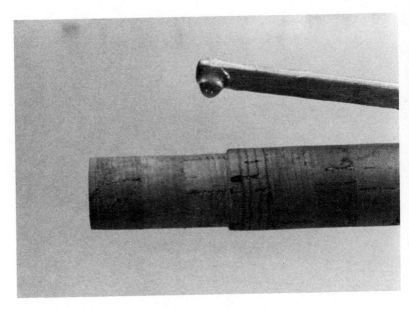

Smear epoxy on the portion of the cork barrel that will be covered by the metal threads.

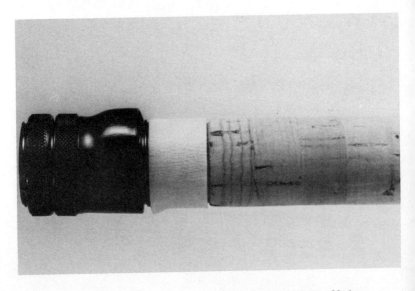

A wrapping of masking tape will keep surplus glue off the threads. Slide the metal threaded part over the cork.

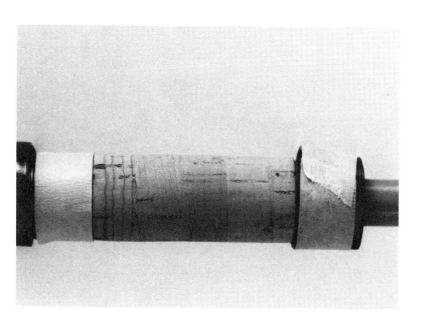

Apply epoxy to the other end of the cork and slip on the metal hood.

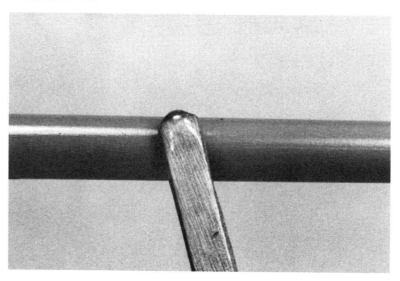

Add a generous amount of epoxy to the portion of the blank to be covered by the handle. Slide on the handle.

Place a dab of epoxy on the front of the cork and cover with
the winding check.

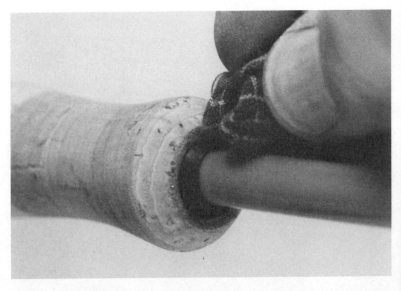

Remove the masking tape. Wipe off any excess glue from the
reel seat, handle, and winding check with a clean rag dipped
in acetone.

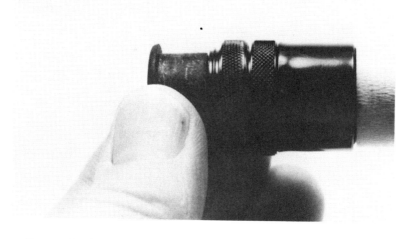

Insert the butt cap. If a fighting butt is to be used with the
rod, the butt cap should not be glued. A little epoxy will
secure it firmly in place.

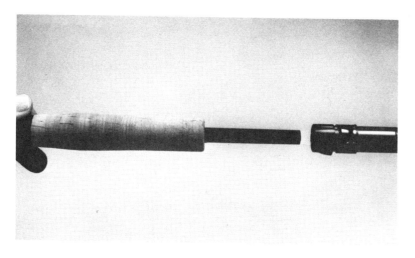

A removeable fighting butt can be made from a portion of
an old fishing rod or even a wooden dowel. Trim the old
blank or dowel until it will go inside the butt of the rod.
Add some cork and a butt cap and the fighting butt is complete.

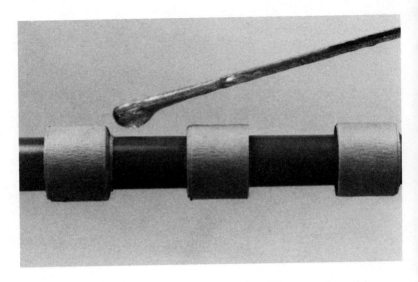

If an all aluminum reel seat is used, several layers of masking tape or a cork bushing may be needed to provide a snug fit. Apply a generous quantity of epoxy to the blank and the tape.

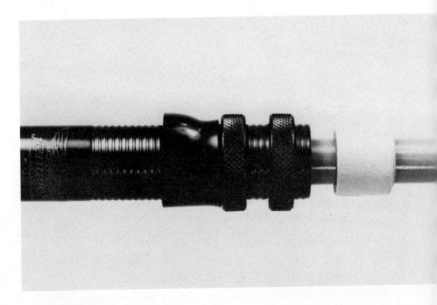

Slide on the reel seat.

Reel seats with wooden barrels may require some reaming with a round file or narrow knife in order to fit over the blank.

There are varying opinions as to whether the fly rod tip top and guides should be on the spine side of the blank or on the reverse side.

Frankly, I cannot tell much difference in the way the rod casts. Tape on the guides and tip top and decide for yourself.

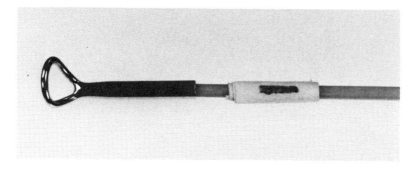

The fly rod tip top can be either the hard chrome or light unbraced ceramic variety.

If snake guides are to be used, they should be hard chromed. The plain stainless steel type will quickly be grooved by the fly line. Ultra-light single foot ceramic are preferred by some.

CHAPTER 8

Casting and Spin Casting Rods

C ASTING AND SPIN CASTING rods are perhaps the easiest rods to build because of the manufactured handles that they utilize.

The sequence of assembly is a little different than other rods. The first step is to glue on the tip top with five minute epoxy. The tip top should be in line with the blank's spine. Next, wrap the guides. Carefully check the alignment of guides with the tip top and apply the finish. If the handle had already been affixed to the blank, rotating the blank in the thread wrapping process would be somewhat cumbersome.

Casting rods can be built with either fixed or removeable handles. There is not much to be gained in the portability of these usually short rods by building them with detachable handles. The handles sometimes work loose and the reel drops in the mud or the handle is lost.

The surest bet is to epoxy the handle to the rod blank. Manufacturers of casting handles make various sizes of adaptors to fit the different diameters of the butts of the blanks. Before beginning the gluing, assemble the adaptor and the parts of the handle on the blank.

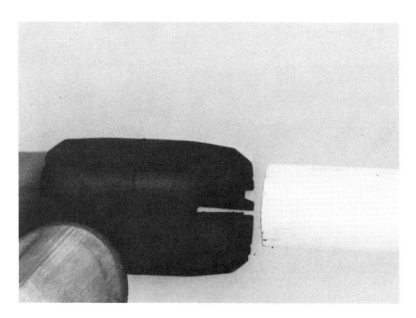

Slide the forward portion of the handle up the blank.

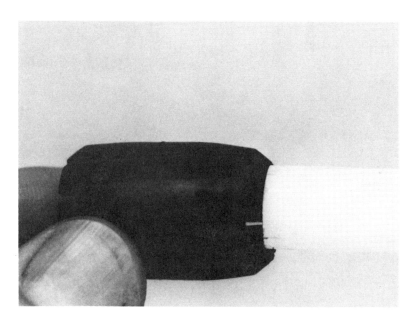

Apply epoxy to the butt of the blank. Slide on the adaptor.

Smear epoxy over the outside of the adaptor and slide the forward part of the handle over it.

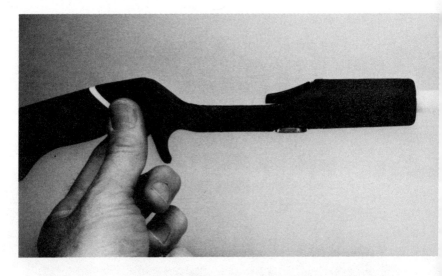

Add a little epoxy to the joining threads of the handle and screw the parts together. Before the epoxy has a chance to set, align the reel seat with the guides and the tip top.

There are other designs of casting handles available. Follow the manufacturer's instructions for proper assembly. If a detachable handle is desired, glue only the adaptor or butt ferrule to the blank.

CHAPTER 9

Some Thoughts on Guides

B OAT RODS ARE SUBJECTED to hard use. Heavy duty hard chromed or ceramic guides are in order. The braced types may be necessary for handling large fish.

Trolling rods generally require a roller tip top. If wire line is going to be used, roller guides are essential.

Surf rods are frequently used to propel heavy weights long distances. The large spinning guides used should be the braced type.

Strong pressure is often needed to wrench uncooperative bass from the brush with the Flippin Stick. Heavy duty guides and tip top are required. Except for exceptionally stiff bass rods, the standard ceramic guides and tip tops perform very well. The combination of very heavy line and a stiff rod demands braced guides.

59

CHAPTER 10

Guide Wrapping

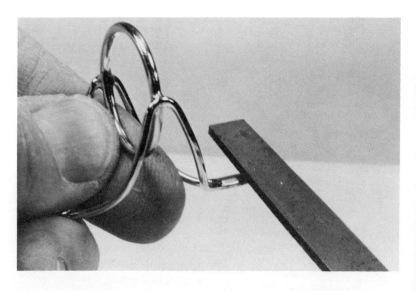

As they leave the factory, rod guides have blunt, rough feet. In order to have an even flow of thread from the blank to the guide, the feet of the guide must be tapered and smoothed with a file or hone. If the guide foot is rough, the wrapping thread will be frayed or cut. Be sure to smooth the underside of the guide foot as well as the top.

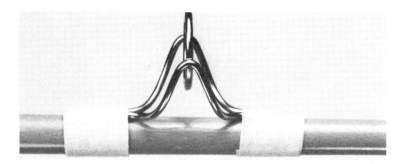

Tape the guides to the blank. When the rod is bent, guides should be spaced so that the line will not rub against the blank. This is especially critical on rods that use casting or spin casting reels and have the guides on top. Adjust the suggested guide spacing if necessary.

When the guides are spaced to your satisfaction, it is time to begin the wrapping. An adequate thread tension device can be made from a book, milk jug and a cup. Experiment a little to determine the correct amount of tension on the thread. The guide should be slightly moveable after one foot is wrapped. If the guide cannot be moved, too much thread tension has been used. Tension on the thread can easily be adjusted by increasing or decreasing the amount of water in the jug.

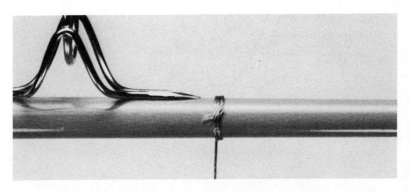

Remove the tape from one foot of each guide. While holding the free end of the thread against the blank, rotate the blank and wrap the thread over itself. After a few turns, cut off the free end of the thread. Keep rotating the blank until the wrap is eight or ten turns from being complete.

Great care must be taken not to let the thread climb over previous wraps. Use your fingernail or a toothpick to push the thread up snugly to previous winds.

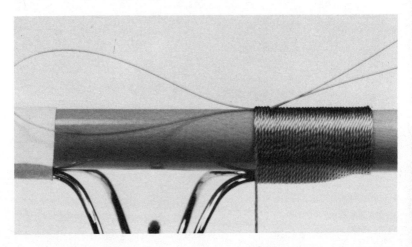

Lay a loop of six or eight pound test monofilament on the blank and rotate until the wrap is complete.

Cut the thread and pass the tag end through the loop. Pull the loop through the thread wrapping and the thread will be buried under itself.

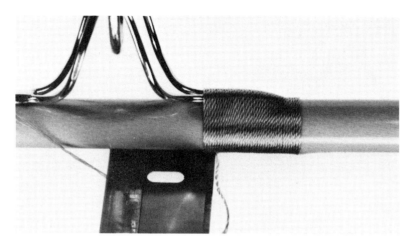

Carefully trim the thread. Wrap the same side of the guide feet on all the guides.

As soon as all of the guide feet on one side of the guides are wrapped, remove the tape from the guide feet on the other side of the guides.

Check the alignment of the guides with the tip top.

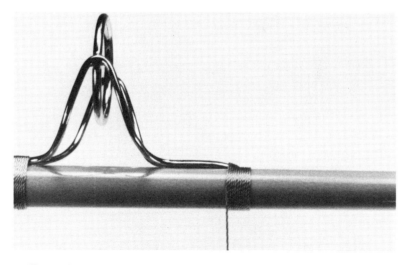

Turn the blank end for end and wrap the other guide feet. Care should be taken to make the wrap on both feet of the guide identical.

63

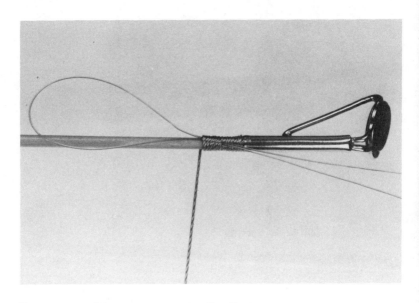

Place a matching wrap next to the tip top.

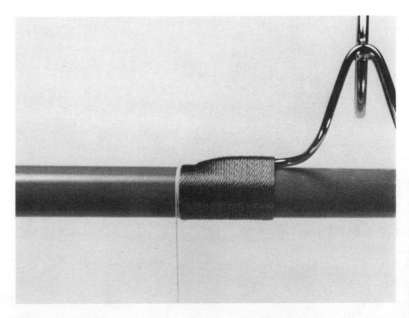

Most rod builders like to trim the thread wrap with a
harmonizing or contrasting color of thread.

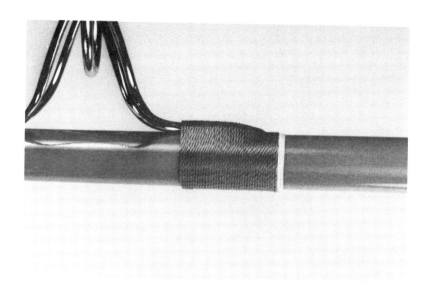

Choosing a smaller sized thread for the trim will result in a
nice tapered effect.

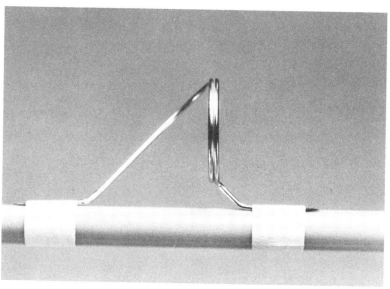

If foulproof guides are used, remember that they are direc-
tional. The butt guide on the rod would be placed this way
with the reel seat to the right.

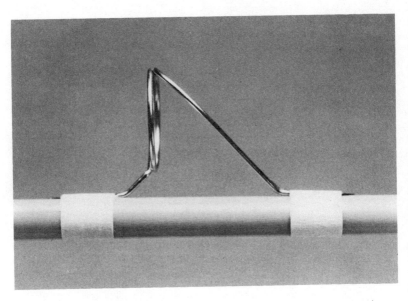

The rest of the guides on the rod would face this way. Again, the reel seat should be to the right.

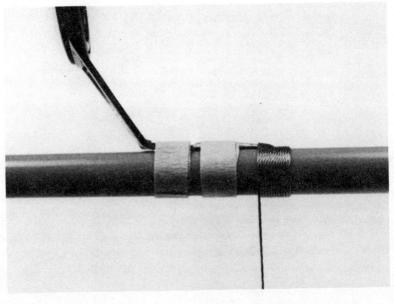

Single foot guides can be secured with a couple pieces of tape.

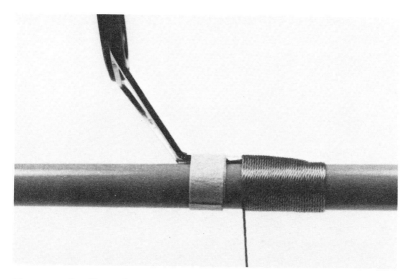

Remove the first piece of tape as the wrapping proceeds up the foot of the guide.

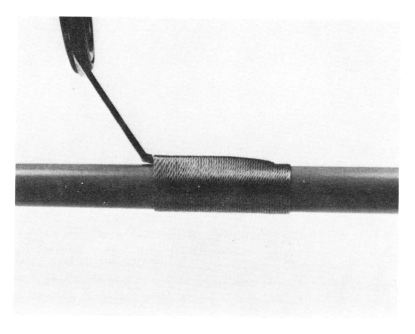

Tie off the wrapping in the regular manner.

Some rod builders believe that if a rod is going to be subjected to heavy strain the guides should be double wrapped. The reasoning is that the underwrap will prevent the guide feet from biting into the blank.

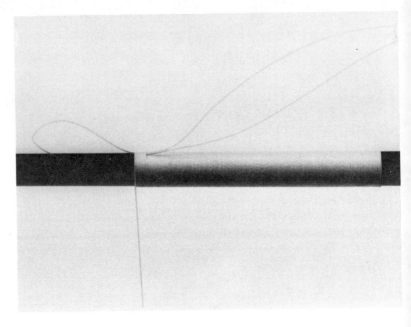

If a double wrapping is desired, measure the length of the guide from foot tip to foot tip. The underwrap should be about 1/4 inch longer than this measurement. The overwrap will be smoother if the underwrap is done with size A thread.

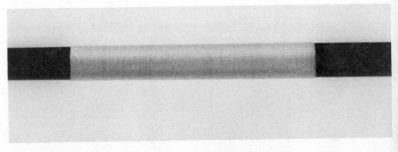

Give the underwrap a coating of thread finish.

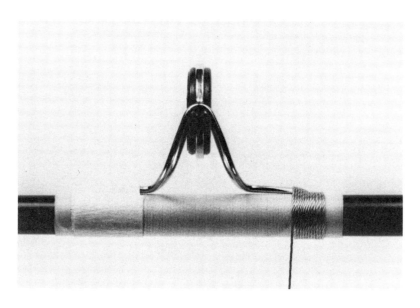

When the underwrap's finish is dry, wrap the guide in the regular manner. A word of caution: double wrapping the guide adds considerable weight to the rod and should be done only when a fairly stiff blank is used.

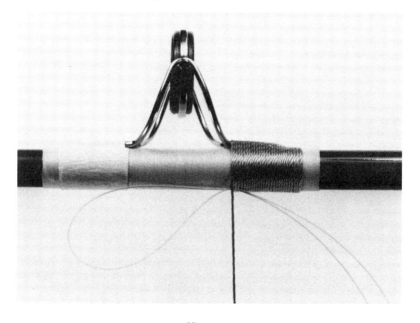

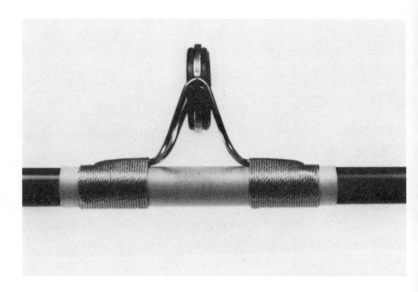

After the overwrap is completed, apply finish to both the overwrap thread and the exposed underwrap.

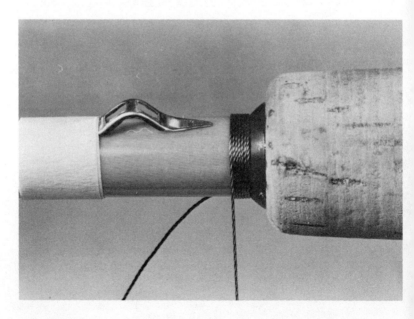

If a hookkeeper is desired, wrap it next to the winding check.

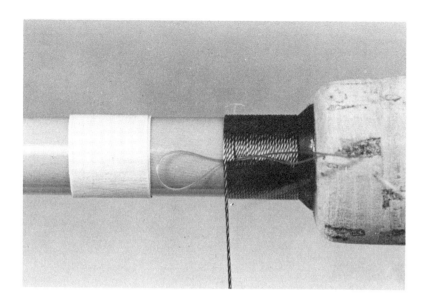

If a hookkeeper is not used, a few turns of thread that match
or harmonize with the guide wraps will insure a finished
look next to the handle.

Some custom rod builders like to fancy up their rods with
intricate and complicated butt wraps. Chevrons, fish, flags,
names and many complex designs are used. A complicated
butt wrap does not make a rod fish better. Multi-colored
butt wraps can be an art form. If these appeal to you, try
some experimental wraps on a piece of rod blank. My big-
gest objection to them is that they add unnecessary weight
to the rod.

SUGGESTED GUIDE SPACING FOR STEELHEAD AND SALMON RODS
(All Measurements in Inches)

Note: Bottom figure is guide size.

Rod Length		Tip top to 1st guide	2nd	3rd	4th	5th	6th	7th	8th	9th	Butt guide to reel seat
7'9"	Spinning	6	13	22	32	43	57				19
		10	12	16	20	25	30				
8'	Spinning	5	12	21	32	45	60				19
		10	12	16	20	25	30				
8'3"	Spinning	5	11	17	25	33	43½	56½			25
		8	10	12	16	20	25	30			
8'6"	Spinning	4½	11	18	26	34½	46	60			24½
		8	10	12	16	20	25	30			
8'9"	Spinning	5	13	22	33	47	62½				26
		10	12	16	20	25	30				
9'	Spinning	6	13	21	30	40	50¼	63			27
		10	12	16	20	25	30	40			

CASTING RODS:

Rod Length		Tip top to 1st guide	2nd	3rd	4th	5th	6th	7th	8th	9th	Butt guide to reel seat
7'6"	Casting	3½	7½	12	17	23	31	40	51		22½
		6	6	6	6	8	8	10	12		
7'9"	Casting	4	8½	13½	19	25½	33½	43½	57		19
		6	6	6	6	8	8	10	12		
8'	Casting	4½	9½	14½	20½	27	34	43½	56½		22½
		6	6	6	6	8	8	10	12		
8'3"	Casting	3	6½	10½	15½	22	29	37½	47½	61	21
		6	6	6	6	8	8	8	10	12	
8'6"	Casting	3	6½	10½	16	23	29½	38½	49½	64	22
		6	6	6	6	8	8	8	10	12	
8'9"	Casting	5	10½	16½	23½	31½	40½	50½	62		27
		8	8	8	8	10	10	12	16		
9'	Casting	4½	9½	14½	21	29	38½	51	67		24
		8	8	8	8	10	10	12	16		

SUGGESTED GUIDE SPACING FOR SPINNING RODS
(All Measurements in Inches)
Note: Bottom figure is guide size.

Rod Length	Tip top to 1st guide	2nd	3rd	4th	5th	6th	Butt Guide to Reel Seat
4'6"	4½	9½	18½	28½			17½
	6	8	10	12			
4'9"	5	11½	20½	30½			18½
	6	8	10	12			
5'	5½	13	22½	34½			17½
	6	8	10	12			
5'3"	5	11½	19	27	36½		17½
	6	8	10	12	16		
5'6"	5	11	18	26	37		22
	8	10	12	16	20		
6'	5	11½	21	32	45		17½
	8	10	12	16	20		
6'6"	4½	10	17	25	36	48	17
	10	12	16	20	25	30	
7'	5	11	18	27	36	48	24½
	10	12	16	20	25	30	
7'6"	5	12	21	31	42	55	24½
	10	12	16	20	25	30	

SUGGESTED GUIDE SPACING FOR FLY RODS
(All Measurements in Inches)
Note: Bottom figure is the snake guide size.
The butt guide size is a two-footed ceramic.

Rod length	Tip top to 1st guide	2nd	3rd	4th	5th	6th	7th	8th	9th	10th	11th	12th	Butt guide to reel seat
6'	4	9	15¾	23½	31½	40							28
	1	1	1	2	2	8							
7'	4½	10	16½	24	32½	42	52½						27
	1	1	1	2	2	2	8						
7'6"	4½	9½	15½	22½	30	38½	48½	59					27
	1	1	1	2	2	2	2	8					
8'	4½	9½	15½	22½	30	38½	47½	56½	66				25½
	2	2	2	2	3	3	3	3	10				
8'6"	4	9	15	22	30	39	49	60	71				26½
	2	2	2	2	3	3	3	3	10				
9'	4½	9½	15½	22	29	36½	44½	54	65	76			27
	3	3	3	3	3	4	4	4	4	12			
9'6"	4½	9¼	14½	21	28½	37	47	57½	70½	83			26½
	3	3	3	3	3	3	4	4	4	12			
10'	4½	9½	15½	21¾	29	37	46	55¾	65	77	89½		25½
	3	3	3	3	3	3	4	4	4	4	12		
10'6"	4½	9½	15	21	27½	34½	42	50	59	69½	81	94	27½
	3	3	3	3	3	3	4	4	4	4	4	12	

SUGGESTED GUIDE SPACING FOR OTHER TYPES OF RODS
(All Measurements in Inches)
Note: Bottom figure is guide size.

Rod Length		Tip top to 1st guide	2nd	3rd	4th	5th	6th	7th	8th	Butt guide to reel seat
5'6"	Boat Rod	3½	7½	12½	17½	23	29			21
		8	8	10	10	12	16			
6'	Boat Rod	4	8½	14	21	29	38			19
		8	8	10	10	12	16			
6'6"	Boat Rod	3½	7½	12	17	23	29	36		25
		8	8	8	10	10	12	16		
7'	Boat Rod	3½	7½	12	17	23	29	36	45	21½
7'	Trolling Rod	7	14	22	32	46				20
		10	10	10	12	16				
10'6"	Surf Rod	8½	19	33	49	71				29
		10	20	30	50	75				
7'6"	Flippin' Stick	5	11	18	26	35	45			32
		8	8	10	10	12	16			
5'6"	Light Action Casting	4	8½	14½	21½	29½	38			17½ to Handle
		8	8	8	8	10	12			
5'6"	Heavy Action Casting	5	11	18	27	37				18 to Handle
		8	8	10	10	12				
6'	Casting	5	11	18	26	35½	46			15½ to Handle
		8	8	8	10	10	12			

CHAPTER 11

Ferrule Wrapping and Miscellaneous

T HE MOST CRITICAL part of the self ferruled tip over butt blank is the leading edge of the female portion. This edge will be subjected to much pressure as the rod is flexed while casting or fighting a fish.

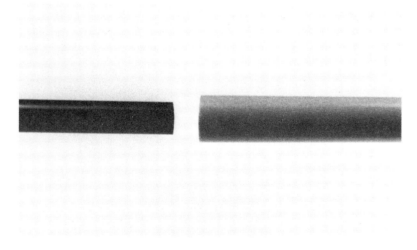

It is important that this portion of the blank is double wrapped. Begin by inserting the butt section of the blank into the tip section. It is a little handier if you can use a short section of scrap for this purpose.

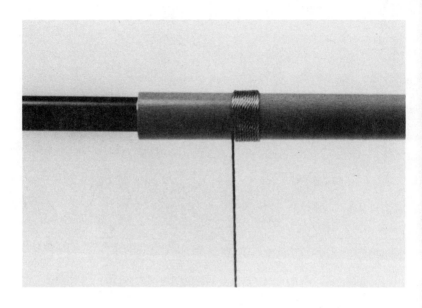

The wrap is started about two inches from the end of the blank.

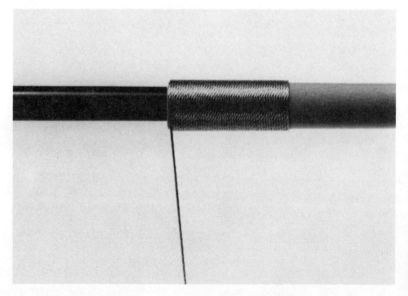

Stop the thread about 1/16 inch from the leading edge of the blank.

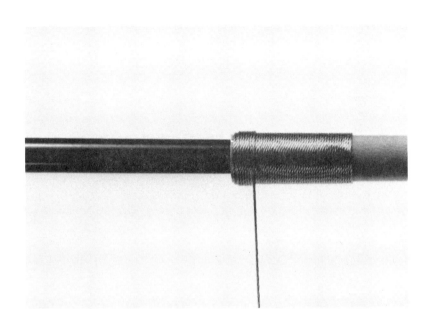

Wrap the thread over itself.

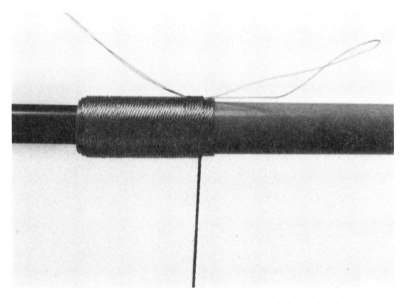

For a tapered effect, stop the thread about 1/8 inch before
coming to the starting point.

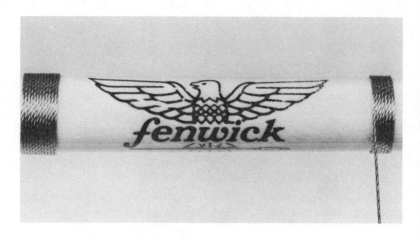

If desired, the name of the manufacturer of the blank can be framed with a thread wrapping.

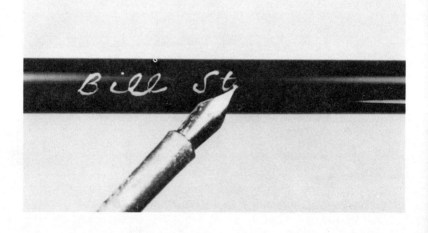

The name of the owner along with the specifications of the rod can be written on the blank. India ink, exterior latex paint or hobby shop type enamel may be used for this purpose. Very fine steel wool is used to slightly roughen the surface where the writing will take place. A coating of the thread finish will permanentize the inscription.

CHAPTER 12

Applying the Finish

B EFORE APPLYING THE finish to the thread, sight
down the rod and make sure the guides are in line with
the tip top and reel seat.

Check each guide wrap.

Very carefully read the directions printed by the manufacturer of the thread finish.

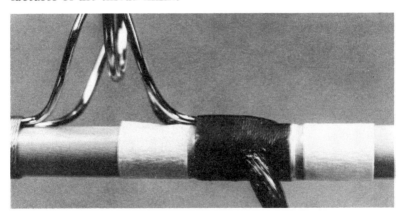

Masking tape will insure a smooth job.

Clean your brush with acetone before applying color preserver or the final finish to the thread. Rotate the blank
while applying the finish. If the finish starts to thicken in its
container before the job is complete, discard it and mix a
fresh batch. Clean the brush with acetone and continue.

Remove the masking tape as soon as the thread coating
is completed. If the masking tape is allowed to remain on

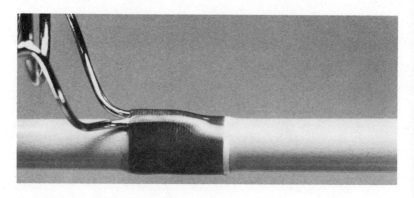

the rod until the finish is dry, a sharp ridge at the edge of the finish will result. As soon as all the wraps have been covered, grasp the rod by its handle and carefully proceed to your TV set. While watching a program or two, slowly revolve the rod in a horizontal position. This step will prevent the finish from sagging.

Most folks cannot resist touching the finish in order to determine if it is dry. Dab a little of the finish on a piece of scrap or block of wood as you begin to cover the wraps. This test area can be touched whenever desired and your beautiful rod will not be smeared.

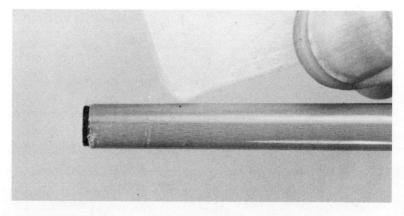

The final touch is to rub a little paraffin on the male portion of the ferrule. This will insure a tight fit.

You have done it! It's time to go fishing!!